SOLVING THE WORLD'S PROBLEMS

Solving the World's Problems

Poems

Robert Lee Brewer

Press 53
Winston-Salem

Press 53, LLC
PO Box 30314
Winston-Salem, NC 27130

First Edition

A TOM LOMBARDO POETRY SELECTION

Cover design by Kevin Morgan Watson

Cover art, "Orange Notes in December" Copyright © 2013
by Nicki Fitz-Gerald, used by permission of the artist.

Author photo by Simon Brewer

Back cover author photo by Tammy Foster Brewer

Printed on acid-free paper
ISBN 978-1-935708-90-2

for the living

Acknowledgments

Many of the poems (or versions of the poems) in this collection
have been previously published (or accepted for publication) in
the following publications:

Denver Syntax, "i bet he writes her those poems"; "someday i may
find my life reflected in a mirror"
Escape Into Life, "a small tear in the pillow"; "cold water"; "i'm
learning to listen"
Foliate Oak, "the horizon is marked by water towers overlooking
trees"
Ghost Ocean Magazine, "dozen fortune cookies"
Hobble Creek Review, "accident vehicles"; "murder & the love curse"
Kind Over Matter, "i think the world is a pin cushion"
La Fovea, "one day we looked for the snow"
MiPOesias, "anywhere we dare go"; "church"; "watching the ice
melt"; "wild-eyed eskimo dream"
OCHO, "solving the world's problems"
Otoliths, "anatomy of a pencil"; "follow me like bright stars"; "like
apple cider spiked with spirits"; "why i never mention the traffic
report"
Poetry Bomb Project, "the last bomb on earth"
Remark, "buried alive"
The Smoking Poet, "this is modern living"
Words Dance, "my sinister is sparking"; "you origami me"
Zygote in My Coffee, "relevant"

Thank you to every editor and publisher who has shown faith in
my work. So much. You kept the wick lit when I needed it most.

Solving the World's Problems

III

INTRODUCTION
by Tom Lombardo, Poetry Series Editor

Robert Lee Brewer, the Poet Laureate of the Blogosphere in 2010, has been a central figure in both on- and off-line poetry for more than a decade. As an editor for *Writer's Digest*, he's written and presented more poetry to wider audiences of which most poets may only dream. He's well-known to more poetry lovers than anyone this side of Billy Collins, and he's published his poems widely in print and electronic formats. *Solving the World's Problems* is his first full-length collection, and I'm honored to present it to you.

The collection opens with a poem that presents one long existential question

> *what's more important*
> > *writing a poem*
> > > *or building a bridge*

then bounds through a Tolkien tale of chairs, stores, trucks, assembly lines, trees, and lumberjacks—there and back again—until Brewer knits it when

> *poets consider which chair*
> > *is going to inspire them*
> > > *to write* the *poem*

Brewer uses his own chair very well. In *Solving the World's Problems*, he's created a book-length collection that boldly examines—with the same intricate interconnections as his poet's chair—how the relationship we call love works, starting with where and how we find it when we're looking for it.

> *… a love that always exists somewhere*
> *else*
> > *hidden in the spaces between*
> *…*
> > > *we follow it*
> *until we find a field filled with fireflies*

Once found, the basis for an early love relationship is desire—pure, unadulterated human, sexual desire.

i remember which angle the sun
         took to surround your face with fire
      and the birds bombarded the beach

with the sound of their wanting
...
she slipped out of her slip   she left
            it on a bench and then asked me
      to follow   her bells became stars

when the boomerang moon melted

Once consummated, the relationship grows and matures and along the way rivers, mountains, chasms, galaxies must be bridged. Brewer shows that sometimes the bridges hold, sometimes they collapse. The moon and stars continue to play a role as well as metaphor, irony, and allusion.

i remember when the water
         was free and our planet fell
from the galaxy

once the moon was a ghost haunting these fields
      a confirmation of things to come   now
            the moon's a rock surrounded by darkness

Brewer's diction and syntax are smoothly objective and self-deprecating, so he stays balanced on the edge of the razors embedded in these poems. But also in Brewer's world there is some hope for some of us. In a 21st Century twist on the 1930s Broadway theme, "Boy meets girl, boy loses girl, boy gets girl," Brewer's arc rises, peaks, and falls as lovers meet, lovers break up, lovers come to some mutual accommodation as partners in this too short, too lonely life, and we still call it love.

the moon a deflated balloon
the stars mere punctuation marks
signaling natural pauses
...

and a little
distance just might
save us both

But in a twist on the fortune cookie poem, Brewer wipes the slate clean.

Ignore all previous fortunes
...
You can start again

Brewer's rhythms and language are lyrical in ways reminiscent of the Romantic poets. But his style is modern and his stories contemporary. These poems may be what Keats or Shelley would write were they alive today. It's a must read for anyone who's ever been in love and understands that a relationship, like...

...a poem is a bomb
waiting to explode

Robert Lee Brewer explodes them both—and explores the fragments—in this dynamite of a collection.

matters of great importance

what's more important
    writing a poem
        or building a bridge

or building a chair
    for people to rest or
        resting on a chair

and thanking the person
    who built it or driving
        a truck loaded with chairs

built by an assembly line
    that creates 1,000 chairs
        or managing 1,000 trucks

that deliver chairs
    and collections of poems
        written by people

who appreciate their chairs
    and the poems
        of other people

i'm sitting in a chair
    this very moment writing
        a poem and wondering

about the people who build
    chairs and drive trucks
        and the people who

orchestrate entire processes
    from felling trees
        to slotting legs into seats

and packing them in boxes
               and driving them over
                              bridges to stores where

poets consider which chair
               is going to inspire them
                              to write *the* poem

that inspires other people
               to build chairs and
                              drive trucks and write poems

I

cold water

we spill ourselves all over ourselves
        our excess light
                our forgiving natures

once we wandered the creek together
        forecasted our futures
                bright and tightly spun

of course we unraveled and marveled
        at our unraveling
                trying to put a name to it

when we failed we created a myth
        passed it to our children
                who reached out eager to see

as they departed to who knows what
        we ached for the creek and our futures
                running across the wet stones

smooth and round   but when we found
        the water again we bent at the bank
                all of us afraid to enter

when we write about love

we don't stare at walls
lost in every errant word
                every closed fist

whether by ocean
or outer space
                in this ship

i write there are no
other eyes
                other hands that travel

the way yours travel
lay across
                these tracks

scream for help
in my dreams
                i'll save you

church

saturday nights in clifton are spent
in attic lofts drinking apple cider
staring at ceiling fans spinning

on a wheel along railroad tracks
that go anywhere which really means
nowhere because we can't decide

what to do with our lives between
classes we may or may not attend
depending upon whether

the cider makes us sick
in the middle of the night
or if we just don't feel

like untangling from whoever
happens to be in our beds
when the alarm sounds

witches dance at midnight

bid farewell to the day that has passed
& welcome the day as it begins
say *we'll be ready when you finish*

cackle with pleasure
cast spells in the darkness
without worrying over good or bad

demand a witness
blind to your desires
command the earth & the fire

obey the whispers of children
& tempt the hearts of lovers
hover over their houses as they sleep

from one place to the next

first there's a girl who visits this playground
on rainy days   today she finds a dead
blue jay and buries it beneath woodchips

several men wearing fluorescent vests
gather around the flatbed of a truck
none of them notice me when i depart

the girl finds a blue feather to insert
into the fresh grave   she bends down and calls
me over   she asks me to say something

i want to say something important   more
than i've ever wanted anything but
i can't find the words   stunned i find my car

leaves flutter from the roof as i drive home
only yesterday they fell from their trees
spiraling to the earth like accidents

alone in the city

she stood at her window
without her shirt   i watched
from below surrounded by snow

even at night everywhere
was light reflecting off her back
revealed to her

waist   her hair pulled tight
we stood like chaste statues silent
in an empty park   she never

turned to reveal her mark
instead with hands over her head
she stepped into the dark

poem

i'm sorry i chose sleep
over pinning you to paper
                outlining an idea

this morning my head
aches with regret
                to know i held you

so ready last night
only to let you sneak
                out the fire escape

the way that i can be

my lips wandered out the room when she did
        because they are not well-behaved around
                beautiful women   a problem they have

is my tongue does not break the silence well
        unless she makes the first move my lips wait
               and wait though there are times my hands rescue

the whole operation watch them *my hands*
      my fingers grasp and maneuver until
            everything mine brushes against her

everything as if she is paint and
        i'm the paintbrush   but no she's the painter
            and i'm the painting admiring her work

i bet he writes her those poems

i bet he writes her those poems
        knowing she wants him to write more
                so she can trick him into believing

she might return the sentiment
        though he knows she could never
                love him like he loves her she

reserves her heart for another
        and i bet he knows this and
                writes her those poems anyway

apple

i've seen my sisters picked
                placed before too many children
        fumbling with their hungry mouths

sometimes i ache for harvest
                afraid i won't fall very far
        forget your appointment

if you want me
                take me now
        before the weather does

# of summer

place your mask on the counter
                and write me a letter without
      the words *love* or *completely*

i remember which angle the sun
                took to surround your face with fire
      and the birds bombarded the beach

with the sound of their wanting
                in the twilight we listened
      to the waves as they worked

the sand with a methodical
                fervor and we imagined
      ways to welcome the night

at the arboretum

from his box of sweethearts
  he hands her candy that reads
    cutie pie

before eating his own
  wild life
    they walk the paved path

to a pond filled with sleeping koi
  a sign warns
    keep off grass

but she leads him there anyway
  in high school this is where
    he would run

across the frozen pond
  and wander off trails
    and into the summer creek water

he hands her *cloud nine*
  and pops a *chill out*
    he remembers being young

and cold in february
  but a sweater feels just right today
    he thinks

i'm not in high school anymore
  and starts to move
    toward the path

but then
  she touches his arm
    whispers *stay*

always running on e

when the food & the money ran out
we ran out
            looking for a job

but there weren't any
                    that were legal
& didn't require a drug test

                            so we marched
on city hall
            & washington

                        & hollywood
& ended up on beaches bumming money
from people who were better than us

at finding jobs
                they gave us their change
& dirty looks

                while making comments
about how they'd like to quit work
& live on a beach

                    invariably we said
write poetry & your wildest dreams
will come true

                we knew we were lying
but good poetry is told slant
                            what else

could we do
            we were afraid
& lonely

        & low on battery power
for our iPads
        so we climbed back

in our hatchbacks
          & our convertibles
& drove home

        & ordered pizza
with the change we bummed
& thought

        maybe our lives weren't
so bad
    after all

        we still had our health
& our line breaks
        & the envy

of the working class
        who dreamed
of being us

        as we dreamed of being them
surrounded by 6-packs
        & endless sex

& a love that always exists somewhere
else
    hidden in the spaces between

because the night calls us

feral cats sound like witches tonight
            we scare them with our flashlights
they scamper into the shadows

whimper their failed spells
            as we hail other hikers
on this trail we thought

would be empty   we suspect
            they're up to no good
they tell us   *we just felt*

compelled to contemplate
            beneath the stars   our existence
but we know that's code

for *getting high*
            or *screwing around*
or just *screwing*

it's impossible for two couples to be
            on the same path under the same moon
with the same lame *just because* reasoning

the other hikers keep walking
            perhaps talking about us
how we're up to no good

and using code and maybe
            at our age we should
if only because

as the sun sets in the forest

she slipped out of her slip   she left
                    it on a bench and then asked me
            to follow   her bells became stars

when the boomerang moon melted
                    her trail went cold   i tried to find
            which way but only the raven

knows   the moon caught a glimpse of the sun
                    but shadow clouds surrounded her
            there was nothing i could explain

she was naked and i was scared
                    of not having her promises
            not that i could ever keep them

a small tear in the pillow

when my finger finds a hole
        its first impulse is to slide
                through the opening and search

even if by searching
        my finger risks damaging the hole or
                whatever opens the hole to me

or even my own finger
        after all holes are miracles only
                lasting so long and if we don't

search and if we don't risk
        damage to ourselves to our holes
                to our things that open the holes

we know in the dark holes
        of our hearts that someone
                or something else will

anywhere we dare go

the copper scent of a summer shower
                    sends us across our remembered crushes
          left hidden in wet grass and creek water

her skin was soft his hands were strong somewhere
                    a bird cried out as the wind bent branches
          that only barely resisted bending

in the evening you'll recall the stars
                    fell out of the sky and danced around us
          as we only worried about ourselves

like welcome miracles

we saw the space station tonight
        it flashed brighter than
                venus on the horizon

i felt the space between us
        expand and contract
                we made a pact to celebrate

our hands became rockets
        our skin became outer space
                and then lift off and yee-haw

we saw the space station
        but our hands kept not keeping
                to themselves   explorations

like these are not planned
        this space between your face and mine
                this hand sliding down your back

we saw the space station
        tonight it flashed brighter
                than venus on the horizon

follow me like bright stars

let's build something to abandon when we
get restless and eager   a house or car
won't contain us   we'll spill out like foxes

it's evening   no moon   we're walking through
the woods without a flashlight   all hungry
and lost but not complaining   we shed clothes

when we find the water   this river from
the mountain we can't see   we follow it
until we find a field filled with fireflies

you origami me

fold me into animal shapes
                and hold me like paper
            you don't want to tear

i've been here before
                i've waited like money
            and spent myself evenly

across your accounts of love
                the time has come for our withdrawal
            into the pleasures of night

these simple transfers and deposits
                these points of interest
            fold me as you will

and hold me longer still
                i'm not a wolf save when
            that's the only way you'll bend me

my sinister is sparking

stand behind a tree and ring a bell
loud as a thunderstorm
i'll count 1,000 sheep to say

    ready or not
    here I come
and rush to find you

    i'm the reason
you couldn't sleep like oxygen
my fire burning to light you

i love you, i love you

a train whistle fades into evening
the platform you've been guarding
never was attacked

you thought if you waited
but no i never knew
the newspapers covered it up

because no one reads them now
a dog barks at your approach
one more train forces its way

through the night calling
the stars the moon
calling all that listens

II

becomes and unbecomes

belongs and unbelongs   his voice over
        water reckons the unreckoned rattles
against gateways beckons children nearer

with tales remembered and unremembered
        my god his voice speaks and unspeaks whispers
and whimpers commands and consoles   even

now surrounded in darkness he becomes
        something more and less than what he is and
claims to be only what he is   he is

the noises that scare us

the path through the woods the eyes on the field
we hide along the edge and look for each
other   someone has to be bold enough

to uncover and hope no shots are fired
we're not here to find something new   we want
reminded of who we were when the birds

first spoke   our wings dissolve as we age and
we feel the strain but don't know the answers
every promise unfolded we sense

there's a moment to wait and a moment
to reach   the sun disappears behind trees
and we find ourselves escaping again

i'm learning to listen

to the swirling winds of my awkward life
               & not be held prisoner by the sound
       of my own voice   every time a ghost

takes my body   bless this night that won't end
               this conversation headed every
     where & nowhere & don't spare one more inch

or let this fire burn out for i am your
               loose cannon   your phantom limb that dangles
     when every other angle extends

get

we can't let this happen
this thing that's happening
     but it won't stop

our eyes telling our mouths
no yes maybe okay
     don't ever stop

a package to pick up
package to deliver
     never ceasing

a wheel and a wagon
the sand dancing beneath
     a song that yields

we saw a fox last night

i was clawing at your feet
        at your nails
was clawing at your hair

was clawing at your face
                at your eyes
        your eyelashes too

was clawing at your skin
        at your naked lips
was clawing at your breath

was clawing at your beating
                heart
was clawing

man-eater

she picks them up with her hands
and chews   beneath the moonlight
she casts terrible shadows

though the men come anyway
from villages and cities
they dream of conquering her

she waits for them as they swing
torches and pitchforks wanting
to devour every man

she waits and when they find her
she raises them with her hands
opens her horrible mouth

dream

the house is empty
instead a barn
filled with junk

and open spaces
he waits for his wife
and a madman or ghost

who wants him to become
a madman or ghost
who wants him to make

this barn his home
but then there is a car
outside that may be 100

miles down the road
nearly parked out front
or just passing by

while honking
and he's not sure
if he's in the barn

or the car or his house
even as he reaches
for his wife

tomatoes

you say *epic* & i say
e-pic   you say *island*
& i say *is land*

we visit a tomato stand
          in mid-winter
because we both have

issues with timing
& commerce
               & commence

with our random comments
so content to contend
               with each other

& our brothers   you say
sisters & i say *cyst*
ears   you say *nonsense*

& i say *none since*
          the last time we pushed
the re-set button

murder & the love curse

                    if it helps
remove her shoes
        change her skirt

her way of looking
all serious
                    change that too

change everything
        because everything
                changes

                like erasable memories
her smile in the morning
        her scent on your hands

the silence between us

i remember when water was free
it was in the autumn dali
visited the high   leaves fell from the trees

and trees fell from the earth   we
propped them up on crutches and cheerleaders
covered them in blue tarps before

becoming witches themselves
cut a hole in the ceiling if you adore the sky
we left the city but the crime followed us

to the suburbs   our cheers turned to chants
faster than we'd like to admit
i'm not saying the water should

be free because everything
has a price but i remember
when the water was free

i remember when the water
was free and our planet fell
from the galaxy

i'll tell you now
i had no meaning   each evening
was a chance to be near you

portrait of an early morning couple

leaning against a building
            facing each other
      they say

i'm not happy
            you're not happy
      we are not happy

we were happy once
            but we're not anymore
      and it's nobody's fault

but it still hurts
            to be this close
      yet so far away

she twists her hair
            around her finger and
      stares into the distance

he studies her face
            before punching
      his fist into his leg

relevant

everywhere there's someone
with bigger feet ready to take
                    your lover out

in the city heat
beneath a summer moon
                    in june

soon it will happen
the longing the long forgetting
                    the fretting

over the time and setting
aside a little to untie
                    this shoestring

noose suffocating your heart
an unnatural suspension
                    of belief

in the promise of two feet
eventually finding
                    corresponding shoes

worried about ourselves

we've finally reached the point at which we
    invent reasons to get upset   we cast
        spells on ourselves curse our own conventions

once the moon was a ghost haunting these fields
    a confirmation of things to come   now
        the moon's a rock surrounded by darkness

we praise our new awareness and question
    our motives   we ask why until we run
        short on answers   what happens when we have

time to think   we transform x into y
    and dismiss the existence of z now
        only a letter that signals the end

anatomy of a pencil

i didn't answer the phone when you called
because I was considering the way
the light reflected off

the ferrule as it held
eraser to barrel
a thin shaft

of graphite
wearing
away

this is modern living

a last gasp
a quick breath holding
on for one more day

the end rushes
from us even
as it draws closer

birds huddle on wires
and wait they circle
us like satellites

there must be a better way
to say this
but last night

i knew you'd
already left when
we kissed

dozen fortune cookies

ignore all previous fortunes   all good
things must end   forgive your broken alarm
clock for not waking you   dreams will haunt your

house and your wife   foxes must claw for their
survival   splash in every puddle
push every button   you will wake up

tomorrow   no one can run from his heart
enjoy chaos   the answers are crickets
chirping in the breeze   you can start again

the last bomb on earth

wait
    if you see the button
push the button

        her button
is a dark puddle in a cave
    proper handshake

        she asks who
is delivering the news
        everyone

is delivering the news he says
everyone is looking down
    on the world

trying to figure it out
a poem in a bomb
        a poem is a bomb

waiting to explode
        line breaks & love
    letters ticking tocks

from fragile clocks
        packages
never received

the last one on earth
        poem & bomb
tick   &   tock

i think the world is a pin cushion

there's a space between everyday matters
that makes someone feel every day matters
a breath or sigh in the darkness   we surround

our time with excuses and distractions bind
those we love with commitments when we should be
splashing around in dark puddles while the rain

covers us in nothing more than what it is

one day we looked for the snow

and we couldn't find any
        our sleds became relics
as half the world drowned

           from the melting
     we could've too
if we'd been born along a coast

and refused to leave
       instead we mourned
           the loss and watched

       on our televisions
the slow chaos unfolding
          an inch at a time

       we watched
     we mourned
we ate ice cream

discovery

it's not until the seventh day
        he realizes the birds are just
leaves the flowers are really plastic

        the moon a deflated balloon
the stars mere punctuation marks
        signaling natural pauses

the bed a remote office her
kiss a handshake and her body
        a sweater left by accident

someday i may find my life reflected in a mirror

the answers are
         crickets chirping
   in the breeze

an old man's sneeze
        snot wiped clean
    across his sleeve

why i never mention the traffic report

cover yourself in gasoline
& wait for developing nations
to wage war over who

has the highest bid
to bring you home naked
& hysterical   you

clawing at your own face
& how you held your phone
whispering *we had a blast*

while it blasted
protect your investments
& elections   the lane

you travel within
while listening to commercials
about correcting

your vision   fixing
your face & removing
your hair with those lasers

buried alive

after so much
      rain landslides
          are inevitable

            and a little
                distance just might
                    save us both

wild-eyed eskimo dreams

would i want to dream this stomach
        this head and hand
heavy as my hollow heartbeat

waiting for a damn shame
snow crunch under full moon
        i swallow your bright misery

without water in my belly
i'll tell thee to run frigid
        through security check

points in confusing airports
waiting for a damn shame
        poor excuse

for something terminal

accident vehicles

maybe his was not a hand
instead he traded one sleight for another
        a tree without lights

forest without fire   she finds him but
can't put the pieces together again
the wind scatters them

the end

she walks out of the kitchen
       up the stairs
       and into the bathroom

closes and locks the door
       behind her   never
       to be heard from again

watching the ice melt

I hope God isn't plagued by hope.
—Heather McHugh

we find him sitting on the coast
of antarctica arms wrapped around
his legs and humming to himself

and we know it's him
because well he just lets you
know these things you know

so we ask him
what're you doing anyway
and he just exhales

like he's annoyed
tugs at his chicago cubs ball cap
and sighs

self portrait

a man who doesn't shave
is a man who doesn't take
            himself seriously

is a man who doesn't floss
            enough or turn down
second helpings   mirrors

don't turn me away
from vices but i want
            to be better without

being fixed   some mornings
            i hear the trains and
            think *run* others

i start a fresh load
of laundry and pick up
the razor   there are

            times i feel i don't
exist   you've seen me
disappear in the kitchen

sink to measure my
life in dishes washed
            the best reflections

            cut both ways and
i'm lost in the hum
of these machines

solving the world's problems

i began as eyelashes blocking the sun
and my father was a digital clock
in a dark cave my father counted

out the minutes as i kept myself
from myself   in this way i learned to kiss
years later when i became a horse

i ran the hot blood out of my body
father turned into a dream filled
with fire and a horrible laugh   i

burned into a cloud of smoke
father became a phone call and then
silence   i worried what i might

transform into next   i worried
what i might already be   then
i forgave father

never afraid to die

some days my only goal is to get out
        of bed brush my teeth   even the grocery
                store weighs on me the constant movement

so i write blog posts and status updates
        i feel empty as a trumpet without breath
                and *love burns fields covered in white lies*

so i drive to her house again listen
        to her records and ex-lover stories
                as the lines stack in my head   this is love

nights without sleep whole weeks without hunger
        so i run out for milk bread and human
                contact because i can't control myself

the wolf   its teeth and claws   howls
        at the moon searches for a red fox
                then her stories are not enough and i

break through walls and women until the beast
        releases me and the earth becomes too
                much to bear again our constant movement

betty

my first word was *stop*
        like an abandoned barn
along a state route

i'd make a good haunted
        house   in the morning
the fists start continue

through lunch   strangers come
        to visit pretend we're
friends   my greatest desire

is escape   there's a door
        a window what i'd
do to break them   even

you the same man who
        visits daily i'd leave
you without warning

bury me when i die

i heard it make a sound but i can't see
tomorrow   the days last longer than years
          on mercury   every point in time

lost in a state of transition a chance to watch
traffic escape the heat   she's got
          a good lawyer   american bullfrogs

eat other frogs   my hunger crawls deeper
into the cave of my ribs   the moon
          a bronze coin tonight   if it's easier

hide me beneath the earth   or hell
burn me   i'm hungry enough to eat
          the planet and all its inhabitants

          this frog eat frog world
with flies on the wall please scatter
my ashes in water and punish me

10:15 in a kroger parking lot

he sits with the engine off staring straight ahead
through wells fargo through the next strip mall and the new
half-developed subdivision with prices that

start in the low five-hundreds through mcdonald's and
chick-fil-a through burger king and dairy queen through
thick and thin cats and dogs teenagers in public

parks radio waves and satellite images
carried to you the possibility of you
a number on a graph some outlier who reads

poetry as if reading might even matter
to the man with this weight on his shoulders staring
without any thoughts because his brain's finally

filled past the point of pure saturation and he's
sitting in his car oblivious to the world
outside the store stocked with fresh fruit and vegetables

and diapers and frozen pizza and toothpaste and
deodorant and trash bags and prescription drugs
and his eyes are wet but he is not crying blank

as he feels and overwhelmed as choreographed
cars park and people enter the kroger and leave
the kroger to drive away somewhere without him

like apple cider spiked with spirits

i'm through with being mr nice guy
the time for mud slinging
                              is upon us

there are libraries full of children
exploring new worlds
                              new ways of looking

at the world
                    father led us to this
path and disappeared into the thicket

of things
              it was up to us to press onward
even as the evidence was gathered

the pricks make the world go round
and all the money in the world is not
worth this moment of autumn

                                   the bonfire
crackling and burning up your silhouette
no one uses card catalogues anymore

the horizon is marked by water towers overlooking trees

i'm through with you
and your crayon kisses
smearing our last chances

to wander crooked paths
in august and sing lullabies
to passing cars blue with longing

but i'm through with you
and your burlap intentions
the way nothing ever changes

and nothing seems able to change
i'll always be a teenager at heart
and we could've

but i'm really through with you
because i'll be out dancing
in the fields at midnight

pulling the world closer to me
leaves falling to the ground
birds flying south

dream

she walks into his room and starts
talking about how he's begun to float
it's getting a little out of hand she says

as she ties rope around his waist
he doesn't try to stop her   in fact
he notices his feet have left the ground

completely   *see* she says
good thing i brought this rope
he hopes it isn't serious

as he floats out the window
i have you she says
even if gravity doesn't

he wants to thank her
but he can't remember how to talk
he just rises higher

as she walks beneath him his legs
and arms spread apart   below
she hides in the shadow of his heart

to madison square garden

after midnight
they're coming
elephants

parading through manhattan
& the bars empty
to see

eight of them in a row
followed
by three clowns

one with a flashlight
one a shovel
the other a bucket

totem

we celebrated & sang ourselves & assumed everything
then we fell from the night & the table
watching our best minds splinter

into a thousand networks
a million mega-pixel paintings
& we were too cool to tell them otherwise

we heard the clocks keeping score
the raptors rapped upon our doors
& still we feigned that we were bored

death dropped by
but we weren't concerned
our best words we saved for devices

& line breaks & everything ever after
the laughter tumbled out of us
as the party raged on

we brought along our guns & ammo
decked out in our finest camo
both hiding & revealing the damn o

of the evening reflecting our foggy
intentions   some of us scattered
but the party raged on

some of us dropped but the party
raged on til the break of dawn
you bet the party raged on

& this is when we started to break
the masks we wore our hooded capes
& yearning for a fast escape

from what may never ever be
a chance at immortality
get this

we heard the learned professor
& we read the transformed poet
& we traveled the unkept paths

& all of it made a difference
but none of it mattered
when the money & the food ran out

A Note From the Author

First, I want to thank everyone who's ever encouraged me to write. Often, it was a small moment or a quick comment about my writing that made all the difference in keeping me on the path. The list is so long and includes teachers, friends, family, co-workers, and complete strangers. If you know me, you've probably left an impression. Thank you.

Second, my editor Tom Lombardo was an absolute force in helping this collection transform into its current state. Thank you so much for accepting the collection "as is," but thank you even more for challenging me to take it somewhere completely new.

Third, I want to thank editors and poets who've provided me with an opportunity to discuss and share poetry. I'm sure to miss people on this list, but I want to make sure I at least thank folks like Collin Kelley, Scott Owens, Aaron Belz, Nate Pritts, Sandra Beasley, Didi Menendez, Pris Campbell, S.A. Griffin, David Smith, Bruce Niedt, Walt Wojtanik, Laurie Kolp, Mary Margaret Carlisle, Jeannine Hall Gailey, Sage Cohen, Jane Friedman, Guy Gonzalez, Del Cain, Kristi Weber, Marie Good, Jessie Carty, Nancy Posey, Jane Shlensky, Gil Gallagher, Nin Andrews, Patricia Fargnoli, Helen Losse, Robert King, Khara House, Nancy Breen, Mary Biddinger, Shaindel Beers, Don Bogen, James Cummins, Terry Stokes, Barton Smock, Joseph Mills, Luc Simonic, Jason Neese, Amanda Oaks, Paul Richmond, and so many others. If your name is not on this list, be sure to give me a hard time about it the next time we meet. My memory sucks.

Finally, nothing I've accomplished over the past few years would've been possible without the most amazing person in my life—my wife, Tammy Foster Brewer. In every way, you've been a perfect companion and friend. I love you. So much.

ROBERT LEE BREWER was born and lived his first 30 years in Southwestern Ohio before moving to the sprawl of Atlanta, Georgia. As Senior Content Editor of the *Writer's Digest* Writing Community, he gets paid to edit books, manage websites, create electronic newsletters, craft blog posts, write magazine articles, participate in online education, and speak nationally on topics related to writing and getting published. As a poet, Robert was named Poet Laureate of the Blogosphere in 2010, has been a featured reader at several poetry events around the country, and has found homes for dozens of his poems in online and print publications. He also self-published two limited edition (and sold out) chapbooks of poetry, *ENTER* and *ESCAPE*. As a freelancer, he curates an image-based poetry series for *Virginia Quarterly Review*. As a human being, Robert is married to the poet Tammy Foster Brewer, who helps him keep track of their five little poets (four boys and one princess). Learn more at www.robertleebrewer.com.

Cover artist **NICKI FITZ-GERALD** began her career as an illustrator in London after graduating from Chelsea School of Art in 1997. Her illustration work has been widely published in mainstream and business publications as well as book covers for the UK publisher, the Women's Press.

In 2010 Nicki fell in love with iPhone photography and her iPhoneography was exhibited at the first Eyephoneography Exhibition in Madrid. Her image, "Flamin' Amy," won 4th place in Life in LoFi's Faved of the Year 2011, and in 2013 Nicki won five awards including four honorable mentions in the Mobile Photography Awards 2013. All five were displayed at the Soho Gallery for Digital Art in New York City and the Holcim Gallery near Toronto in Canada. Nicki 's work and her life as "a mom with an iPhone" was featured in the *P1xels'* digital magazine *iPhotographer* in June 2013.

Nicki is founder of the website iPhoneographyCentral.com, which she now co-manages with Bob Weil. In 2013 Nicki co-authored a book with Bob showcasing 45 top iPhoneographers called *The Art of iPhone Photography – Creating Great Photos and Art on your iPhone.*

Nicki now divides her time between her day job, family, the iPC website and iPhoneography. Find more of her work at www.iphoneart.com/users/420/galleries, and www.flickr.com/photos/52982031@N00/.

CPSIA information can be obtained at www.ICGtesting.com
Printed in the USA
BVOW05s1640190516

448559BV00002B/47/P